ESSENTIAL ELEMENTS®
FOR UKULELE

COMPREHENSIVE UKULELE METHOD
MARTY GROSS

Congratulations on completing *Essential Elements for Ukulele - Book 1*, and welcome to Book 2! In this volume, we will continue to build on the basic skills that you have developed. As you practice the songs and exercises found in this book, you will improve your ukulele playing, but more importantly, you will expand your understanding of music.

Be sure to read the explanations so that you clearly understand each new idea and skill that is presented. Take the time to practice the exercises that you find most difficult. As you focus on those tasks, you will see the most improvement in your musical ability. Enjoy the challenge and share your success by playing the songs you learn for others!

—*Marty Gross*

PLAYBACK➕
Speed • Pitch • Balance • Loop

To access audio, visit:
www.halleonard.com/mylibrary

Enter Code
1076-0837-1576-6647

ISBN 978-1-4803-9598-5

Visit Hal Leonard Online at
www.halleonard.com

Contact us:
Hal Leonard
7777 West Bluemound Road
Milwaukee, WI 53213
Email: info@halleonard.com

In Europe, contact:
Hal Leonard Europe Limited
42 Wigmore Street
Marylebone, London, W1U 2RN
Email: info@halleonardeurope.com

In Australia, contact:
Hal Leonard Australia Pty. Ltd.
4 Lentara Court
Cheltenham, Victoria, 3192 Australia
Email: info@halleonard.com.au

CHORD REVIEW

The songs on this page and the next use chords that you learned in Book 1. Play these songs to practice and review your chord formations.

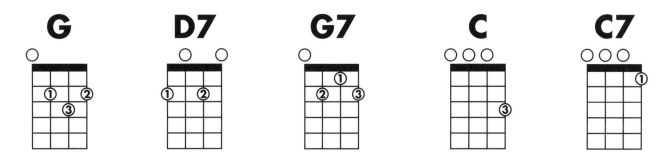

STRUM REVIEW

We'll use this strum to play "Crawdad Song."

1. THE CRAWDAD SONG

Traditional

You get a line, and I'll get a pole, honey.

You get a line, and I'll get a pole, babe.

You get a line, and I'll get a pole. We'll go fish-in' at the craw-dad hole,

hon-ey, sug-ar ba-by, mine.

Check Your Own Progress

- Are you sitting up straight and holding your ukulele correctly?
- Are you strumming down with your thumb and up with your index finger?
- Is your left hand relaxed and curved around the neck of the ukulele?
- Can you move from one chord to another quickly and smoothly?

CHORD REVIEW

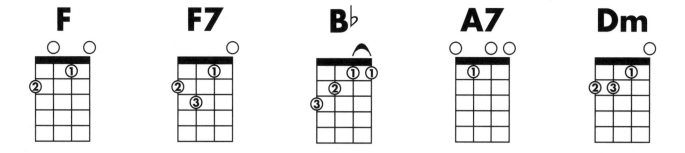

STRUM REVIEW

Use this strum to play "This Little Light of Mine."

2. THIS LITTLE LIGHT OF MINE

Traditional

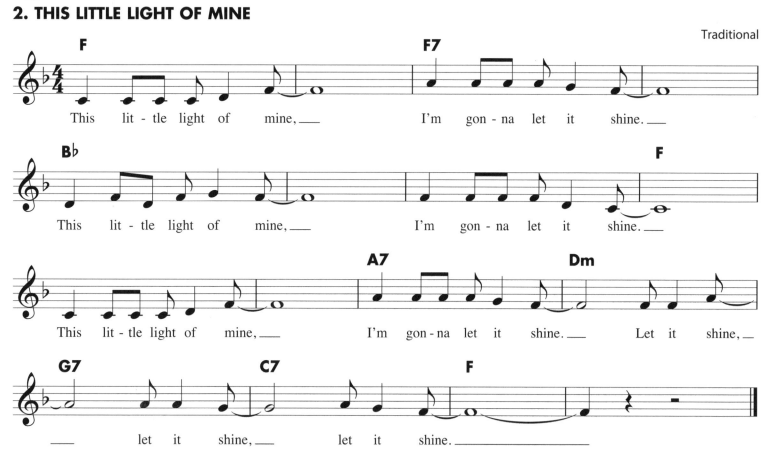

Note Review

In Book 1, you learned how to pick individual notes on the first, second, and third strings to play a melody. Use what you have learned to play the notes for "This Little Light of Mine." Work with a partner, or divide your group in half, to play the melody and the chords together.

CHORD REVIEW

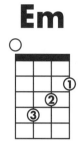

Em

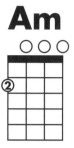

Am

STRUM REVIEW

Use this strum to play "A Hard Day's Night."

3. A HARD DAY'S NIGHT

Words and Music by John Lennon
and Paul McCartney

Verse

C   F   C   Bb   C

1. It's been a hard day's night, and I've been work-ing ___ like a dog. ___ It's been a

F   C   Bb   C

hard day's night; I should be sleep-ing ___ like a log. ___ But when I

Chorus

F   G   C   F   C

get home to you, ___ I find the things that you do ___ will make me feel ___ al - right. ___ When I'm

Bridge

Em   Am   Em

home, ev-'ry-thing seems ___ to be right.   When I'm

C   F   G

home, feel-ing you hold - ing me tight, tight, yeah. 2. It's been a

Verse

hard day's night, and I've been work-ing ___ like a dog. ___ It's been a

hard day's night; I should be sleep-ing ___ like a log. ___ But when I

Chorus

get home to you, I find the things that you do ___ will make me feel ___ al - right. ___

Chord Challenge – Part 1

"This Old Man" can be played using three chords. In the first example, you can use the chords C, F, and G7. Play the first few notes to check your starting pitch and then fill in the chord that belongs in each blank.

4. THIS OLD MAN

Traditional

This old man, he played one. He played knick-knack on my thumb with a

knick-knack, pad-dy-whack, give a dog a bone. This old man came roll-ing home.

Chord Challenge – Part 2

Check the starting notes in this new key signature for "This Old Man." Use the Chords F, B♭, and C7 to fill in the blanks.

5. THIS OTHER OLD MAN

This old man, he played one. He played knick-knack on my thumb with a

knick-knack, pad-dy-whack, give a dog a bone. This old man came roll-ing home.

TABLATURE REVIEW

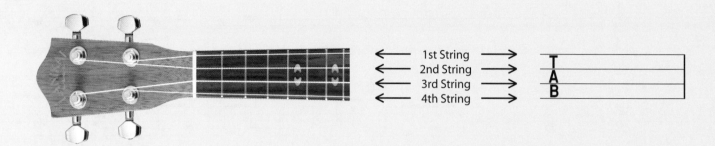

- 1st String
- 2nd String
- 3rd String
- 4th String

- Each line of the tab staff represents an individual string.
- The numbers indicate at which fret to depress the string.
- "0" indicates an open string.

6. JOSHUA (Fit the Battle of Jericho)

African-American Spiritual

TAB QUIZ *Write in the missing numbers and notes to complete both the melody and tablature.*

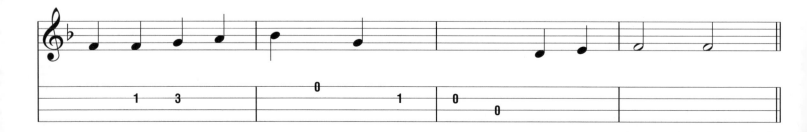

PERFORMANCE SPOTLIGHT

We'll combine what you know about single notes and chords to play a solo ukulele version of "Amazing Grace." Play a single downstroke on the first beat of each measure and use your index finger or thumb to pick the individual passing tones that lead between one chord and the next.

7. AMAZING GRACE – Ukulele Solo

Words by John Newton
Traditional American Melody

PLAYING CHORDS

D
Chord

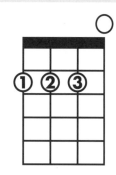

Practice Tip

Play the exercise below and listen carefully to the difference between the new D chord and the D7 chord that you already know. Later in this book, we'll take a more detailed look at what makes each of these chords have its own sound.

8. LUCKY 7

Use this strum to play "This Train."

9. THIS TRAIN

Traditional

1. This train is bound for glo - ry, this train. _____
2. This train don't carry no gam - blers, this train. _____

This train is bound for glo - ry, this train. _____
This train don't carry no gam - blers, this train. _____

This train is bound for glo - ry, don't car - ry no - one but the right - eous and the ho - ly.
This train don't carry no gam - blers, no li - ars, cheat - ers or big shot ram - blers.

This train is bound for glo - ry, this train! _____   this train! _____

PLAYING CHORDS

STRUM BUILDER 1

Use this strum to play "Rock Around the Clock."

10. ROCK AROUND THE CLOCK

Words and Music by Max C. Freedman
and Jimmy DeKnight

PLAYING CHORDS

UNDERSTANDING CHORDS – MAJOR CHORDS

We've been playing chords on the ukulele since the beginning of Book 1. It's now time to take a look at how chords work and what gives each type of chord its own sound. We're going to start by looking at **major chords**. Later in the book, we'll look at minor chords and dominant 7th chords.

Upper case letters are used to indicate a major chord. When you see chord symbols like C, F, Bb, and G in a song, you are playing major chords.

Using what you've already learned by tuning and playing single notes on your ukulele, you can figure out which notes are in each chord.

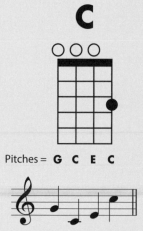

Pitches = **G   C   E   C**

Look at the left-hand formation used for a C major chord. When you strum that chord, you are playing:

- G on the open 4th string
- C on the open 3rd string
- E on the open 2nd string
- C by pressing the 3rd fret on the 1st string

Major chords are always made up of three different notes. Since there are four strings on the ukulele, we normally repeat (or "double") one of the three pitches of the chord. In the C major chord above, the note C is played twice. In this case, we have a low C (open third string) and a high C (third fret on the first string).

When we stack those pitches together, we can see how the C major chord looks when it's written in musical notation:

We can think about these chord notes as part of the C major scale. Major chords are always made up of the 1st, 3rd, and 5th steps of a major scale. Our C major chord contains the notes C, E, and G. In this example, the note C is doubled.

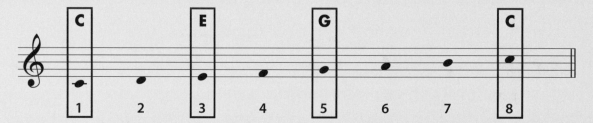

Play the single notes for the C major scale and then strum a C chord. Listen to how the chord notes fit within the scale.

11. C MAJOR SCALE AND CHORD

PLAYING CHORDS

ESSENTIAL ELEMENTS QUIZ – Major Chord Decoder

 On the lines below the chord diagrams, write the names of the pitches that are being played on each string. Then write the notes on the staff. Remember that some chord notes will be doubled.

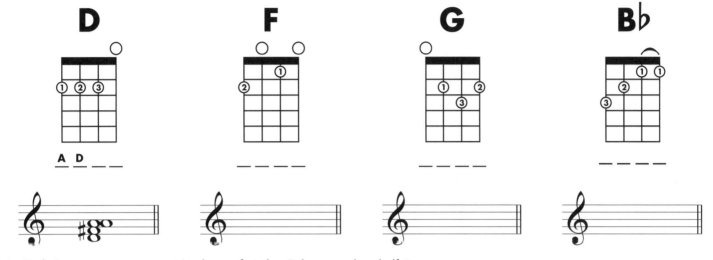

Hint – Each time you move up any string by one fret, the pitch goes up by a half step.

STRUM BUILDER 2

Use this strum to play "Worried Man Blues."

This song contains only major chord sounds.

12. WORRIED MAN BLUES

Traditional

It takes a wor-ried man to sing a wor-ried song. It takes a wor-ried man to sing a wor-ried song. It takes a wor-ried man to sing a wor-ried song. I'm wor-ried now, but I won't be wor-ried long.

PLAYING CHORDS

STRUM BUILDER 3

A **shuffle** or **swing** feeling is an important part of some musical styles like jazz and blues. Instead of playing pairs of eighth notes that divide the beat evenly in half, we make the first note longer and the second note shorter.

In a shuffle style, the first note will be twice as long as the second note. This can give the music a lazy, loping feeling.

We'll use a shuffle strum to play "Sweet Home Chicago." You may not have realized it, but you've already heard the shuffle feel in several songs before this one, including "This Little Light of Mine" and "Rock Around the Clock."

Stop-Time

In order to make a song more interesting, musicians sometimes choose to stop the regular rhythm of the accompaniment and play only a few accented notes. These short silences in the background, or "breaks," draw special attention to that portion of the music. This change in rhythm is common in many styles of music and is also used extensively by tap-dancers.

"Sweet Home Chicago" contains a stop-time section. Pay close attention to the strumming that's indicated.

13. SWEET HOME CHICAGO

Words and Music by
Robert Johnson

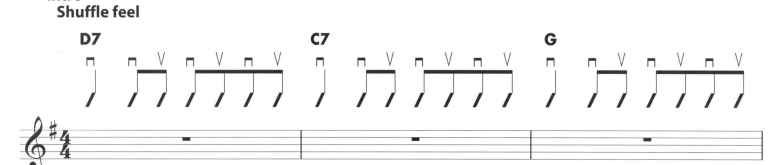

PLAYING CHORDS

Up to this point we've always strummed chords in order to accompany a melody. Another way to create an accompaniment is to use the fingers of your right hand to pick the individual notes of the chord. This style of playing, called **fingerpicking**, is commonly used by guitar and banjo players. There are many variations of fingerpicking patterns and rhythms that can be used. We'll start off with a very basic, repeating pattern.

FINGERPICKING

We'll assign one finger to each string of the ukulele.

- Your thumb (T) will pick the 4th string.
- Your index finger (1) will pick the 3rd string.
- Your middle finger (2) will pick the 2nd string.
- Your ring finger (3) will pick the 1st string.

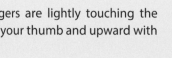

Rest your right hand so that your thumb and fingers are lightly touching the strings that they'll pick. You'll pluck downward with your thumb and upward with your 1st, 2nd, and 3rd fingers.

One string at a time, try picking the pattern T–1–2–3.

Practice repeating that pattern while listening for a steady rhythm, even sound, and equal volume from each string.

For the exercise below, finger each chord formation with your left hand as you fingerpick the T–1–2–3 pattern with your right hand. You'll play the pattern twice for each chord.

14. PICKING PATTERN

T 1 2 3 T 1 2 3   T 1 2 3 *cont.*

HISTORY When the notes of a chord are played one at a time, it's called an **arpeggio**. You might also hear this called a "broken chord." This way of playing chords has been used by musicians for many centuries. You can hear arpeggio patterns used on a variety of instruments in many different styles of music. Banjo players fingerpicking a bluegrass song and harpsichord players performing the music of J.S. Bach in a chamber orchestra are both using arpeggios to create music.

Use the picking pattern that you learned above to play the chords for "Love Me Tender." Work with a partner to play the fingerpicking chords and the melody together as a duet. Trade parts on the repeat so that you practice both. You can expand the arrangement further by having a third player strum each chord with a single downstroke at the beginning of each measure.

15. LOVE ME TENDER

Words and Music by Elvis Presley
and Vera Matson

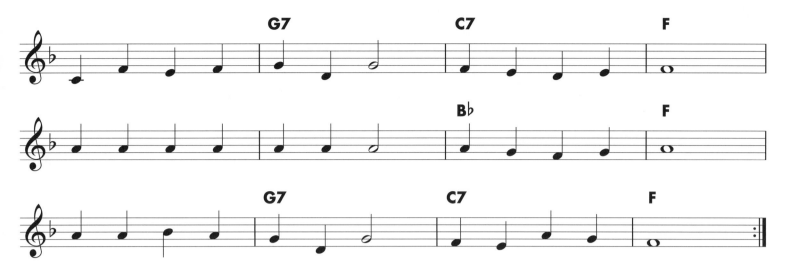

Use the same T–1–2–3 picking pattern to play the repeating chord progression for "All I Have to Do Is Dream." Fingerpick the chords as you sing the melody.

16. ALL I HAVE TO DO IS DREAM

Words and Music by
Boudleaux Bryant

1. When I want you in my arms, when I want you
(2.) I feel blue in the night, when I want you

and all your charms, } when-ev-er I want you ___ all I have to do is
to hold me tight, }

dream, ___ dream, dream, dream. 2. When dream. ___

COUNTING

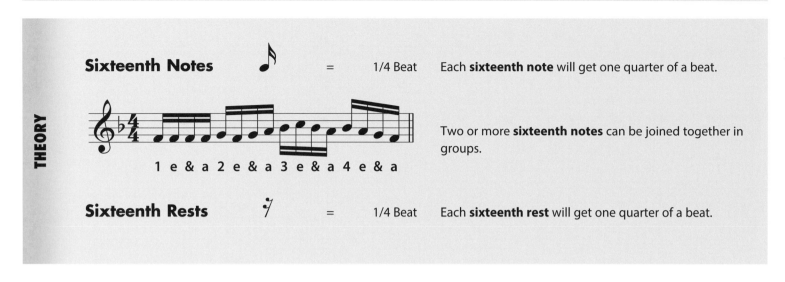

Sixteenth Notes ♪ = 1/4 Beat — Each **sixteenth note** will get one quarter of a beat.

1 e & a 2 e & a 3 e & a 4 e & a

Two or more **sixteenth notes** can be joined together in groups.

Sixteenth Rests = 1/4 Beat — Each **sixteenth rest** will get one quarter of a beat.

Clap and count the examples in the chart below to see how the notes are subdivided into the other rhythms.

4 Quarter Notes =

8 Eighth Notes =

16 Sixteenth Notes =

17. RHYTHM RAP *Clap and count out loud.*

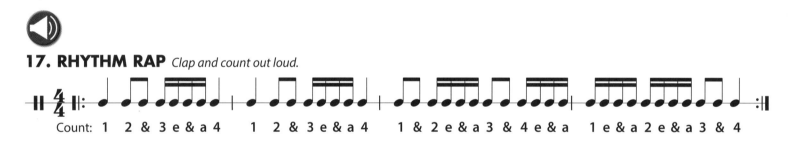

Count: **1   2 & 3 e & a 4   1   2 & 3 e & a 4   1 & 2 e & a 3 & 4 e & a   1 e & a 2 e & a 3 & 4**

18. SASKATOON SERENADE – Duet *Divide into two groups to clap and count this duet. Trade parts on the repeat.*

19. MIXING IT UP *Clap and count the rhythm. Then play the notes of the melody.*

COUNTING

20. CATCH A FALLING STAR *Clap the rhythms while you say the words. Then play the notes of the melody.*

Words and Music by Paul Vance
and Lee Pockriss

Catch a fall-ing star and put it in your pock-et. Nev-er let it fade a - way.

Catch a fall-ing star and put it in your pock-et. Save it for a rain-y day.

Practice Tip

Play these melodies slowly at first to make certain that your rhythms are correct and even. Pick out the most difficult measure and practice it several times to improve your fingering technique. Play the entire melody again a little bit faster. If you have problems at that faster speed, slow down again and work on the small sections that give you trouble.

21. THE GALWAY PIPER

Irish Folksong

22. STEP LIVELY

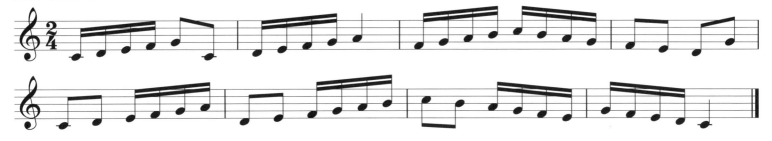

23. FIDDLE TUNE

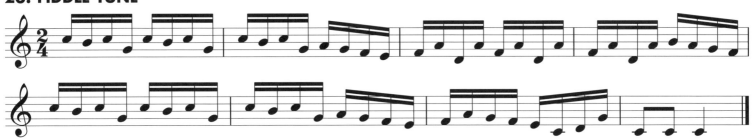

PLAYING CHORDS

Try several different strums from the Strum Chart on page 48 to find a rhythm that works well for "Eight Days a Week."

24. EIGHT DAYS A WEEK
Verse
Shuffle feel

Words and Music by John Lennon
and Paul McCartney

1. Ooh, I need your love, babe, guess you know it's true.
2. Love you ev-'ry day, girl, al-ways on my mind.

Hope you need my love, babe, just like I need you.
One thing I can say, girl, love you all the time.

Chorus

Hold me, love me. Hold me, love me. I

ain't got noth-in' but love, babe, eight days a week.

Chord Challenge

"This Land Is Your Land" can be played using three chords: G, C, and D7. Write in the chords and then choose a strum to play the song.

25. THIS LAND IS YOUR LAND

Words and Music by
Woody Guthrie

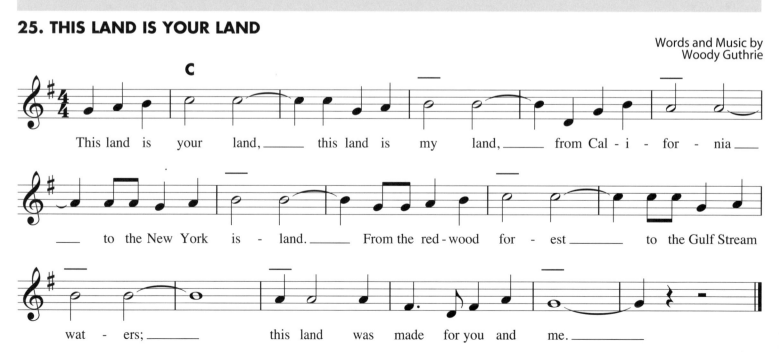

This land is your land, this land is my land, from Cal-i-for-nia

to the New York is-land. From the red-wood for-est to the Gulf Stream

wat-ers; this land was made for you and me.

PLAYING CHORDS

STRUM BUILDER 4

Use what you learned on page 12 about the shuffle style in order to play this strum for "Midnight Special."

26. MIDNIGHT SPECIAL

Railroad Song

PLAYING CHORDS

UNDERSTANDING CHORDS – 7TH CHORDS

Many of the songs you've played on the ukulele use a type of chord called a **7th** or **dominant 7th chord**. Whenever we see a chord name that contains an upper case letter followed by the number "7," it indicates this kind of chord.

Look at the left-hand formation used for a C7 chord. When you strum that chord, you're playing:

- G on the open 4th string
- C on the open 3rd string
- E on the open 2nd string
- B♭ by pressing the 1st fret on the 1st string

Like a major chord, a dominant 7th chord contains the 1st, 3rd, and 5th steps of a major scale. What makes a 7th chord sound different than a major chord is that we add a fourth pitch. This is the flatted 7th step of the scale.

C7

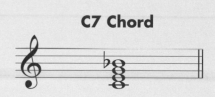

Pitches = **G C E B♭**

C Major Chord

Look at the difference between the C chord and the C7 chord that you play on the ukulele. Play each of these chords and listen to the change in sound.

Dominant 7th chords are described as having a "leading" sound. They sound unfinished and make us anticipate the next chord. We often hear a 7th chord lead us to the final chord of a song.

C7 Chord

Listen to how each of the 7th chords in "Goodnight Irene" leads to the major chord that follows. Stop strumming on the last D7 chord and see if you can sing one or more notes from the final G chord.

27. GOODNIGHT, IRENE

Words and Music by Huddie Ledbetter
and John A. Lomax

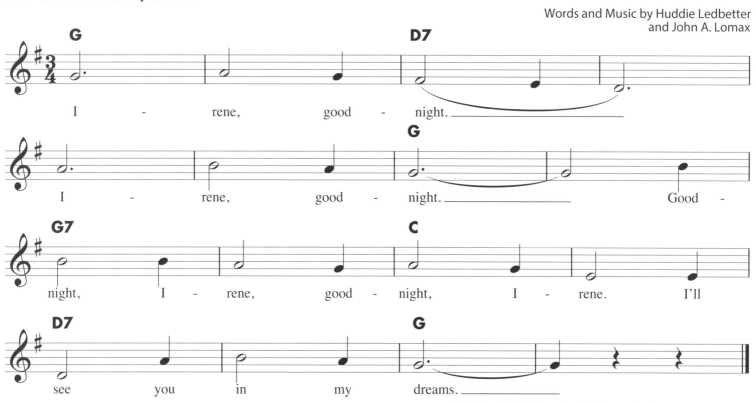

I - rene, good - night. I - rene, good - night. Good -

night, I - rene, good - night, I - rene. I'll

see you in my dreams.

Using What You Know

Go back to page 2 and play "Crawdad Song" again. Find the 7th chords used in that song and listen to how they make the harmony move forward from one chord to the next.

PLAYING CHORDS

STRUM BUILDER 5

You can use a **roll strum** to get a different sound while strumming the ukulele. To play a roll, fan your right hand across the strings, one finger at a time. You'll use the backs of your fingernails to strum the strings. Start with your fingers slightly curled and then open your hand until all four fingers are pointing down. As you open your hand, your 4th, 3rd, 2nd, and then 1st finger will each strum across all four strings. Practice the roll until each strum is a single, even sound.

Use the roll strum on beats 1 and 3 of each measure to play "Shenandoah."

28. SHENANDOAH

American Folksong

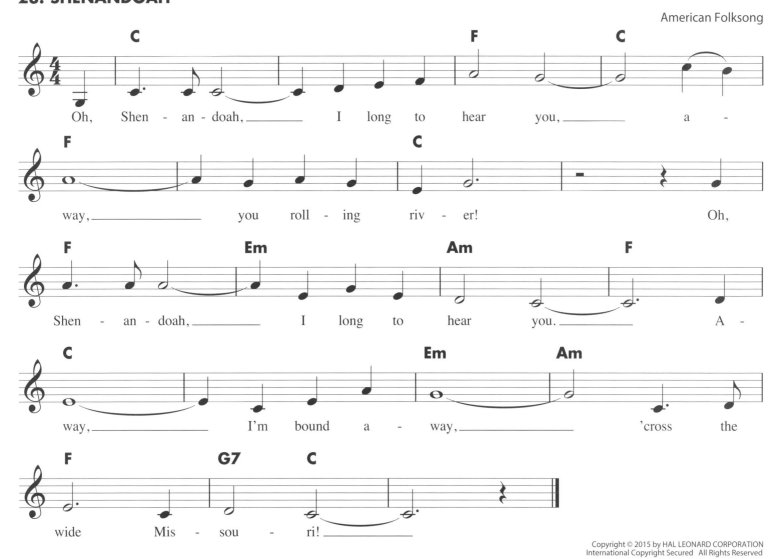

Oh, Shen - an - doah, _____ I long to hear you, _____ a -

way, _____ you roll - ing riv - er! Oh,

Shen - an - doah, _____ I long to hear you. _____ A -

way, _____ I'm bound a - way, _____ 'cross the

wide Mis - sou - ri! _____

NOTES ON THE FIRST STRING

Let's expand our range with two new notes on the first string.

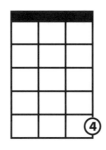

D
5th Fret
4th Finger

D

29. DELIGHTFUL

30. SHALOM CHAVERIM (Goodbye, My Dear Friend) – Round

Traditional Israeli Folk Song

31. THE STREETS OF LAREDO

American Cowboy Song

PLAYING NOTES

Using Your Skills

1. Play the melody for "Wayfaring Stranger."

2. Use the Chord Chart on pages 46 and 47 to learn the new Gm chord that's used in this song.

3. Play the chords and sing the melody.

4. Work with a partner to create a duet of the song. Choose a strumming or picking pattern that expresses the proper mood to match the song.

32. WAYFARING STRANGER

Southern American Folk Hymn

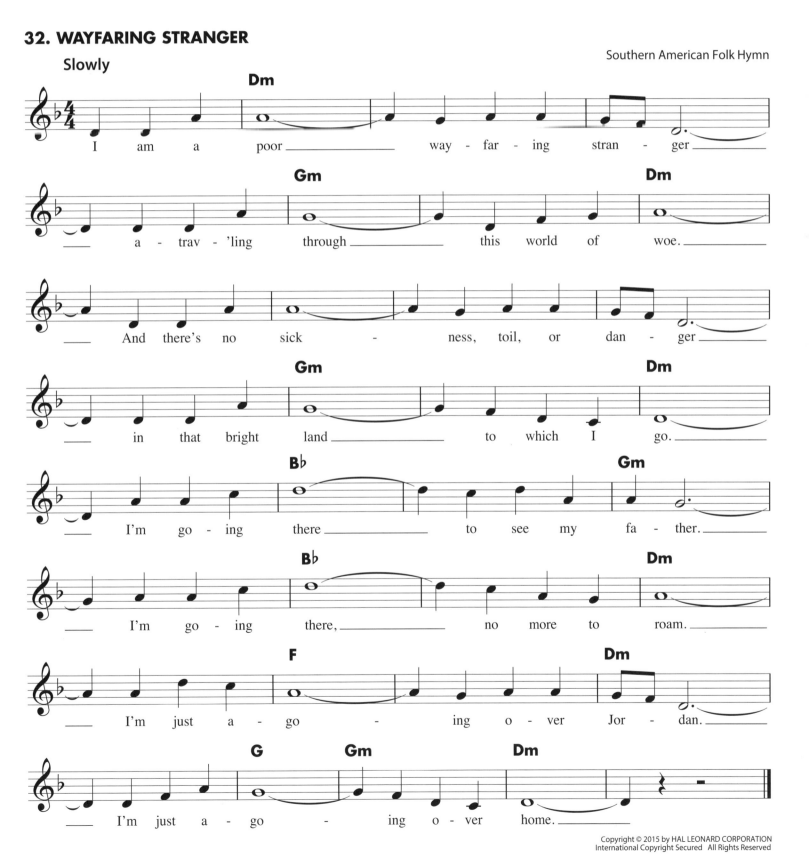

NOTES ON THE FIRST STRING

C#
4th Fret
3rd Finger

C#

Key Signature Review

Sharps and flats can be applied to one note or they can be indicated in the key signature that applies to an entire piece of music. In the key signature shown here, every F would be played as F#, and every C would be played as C#.

For melodies that use the new C# and D, it will be more comfortable to shift your left hand up one fret when you play on the first string. In other words, instead of playing the B with your 2nd finger, you'll use your 1st finger on the second fret.

33. SHIFTING GEARS

Fingers: 1   3   4 3 1

(C#)

34. ROUNDING UP - Round

We've played many songs and exercises that use the C major scale. By using the notes F# and C#, we can now play a D major scale. This allows us to play songs that are based on the D major scale.

35. C MAJOR SCALE

36. D MAJOR SCALE

(F#)   (C#)

NOTES ON THE THIRD STRING

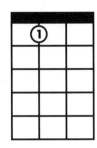 

 ## 37. SIDEWINDER

 ## 38. MINUET

By Johann Sebastian Bach

Transposition

When you move a song from one key signature to another, you are **transposing** the song. Musicians often transpose in order to make a song easier to sing or play.

Play this melody from the song "Shortenin' Bread" starting on the note C.

Now start on the note D and figure out the notes for the same melody. Write the notes on the staff below.

COUNTING

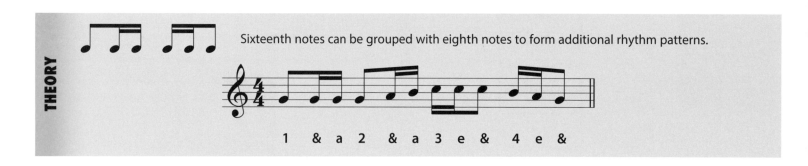

Sixteenth notes can be grouped with eighth notes to form additional rhythm patterns.

1 & a 2 & a 3 e & 4 e &

39. EIGHTH/SIXTEENTH COMBO *Clap and count.*

Count: **1 & 2 & a 3 & 4 & a** *cont.*

40. SEA SHANTY

Can you recognize the two famous melodies used in this duet?

41. DO TELL – Duet

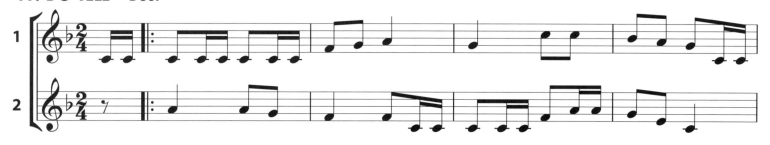

Switch parts on repeat

COUNTING

42. SIXTEENTH/EIGHTH COMBO *Clap and count.*

1 & 2 e & 3 & 4 e &

43. CHESTER A. ARTHUR'S INAUGURAL FANFARE

44. RHYTHM STAR

HISTORY

The song "Rhythm Star" is a **variation** of the familiar song "Twinkle, Twinkle, Little Star." Composers often take a melody, also called a **theme**, and create variations by changing the rhythm, harmony, or style of the piece. Wolfgang Amadeus Mozart, Franz Schubert, Ludwig van Beethoven, and Johannes Brahms are among the many composers who have used theme and variations in their famous works of music. You can also hear musicians creating variations on a melody as they perform jazz.

Count and clap this exercise both forward and backward. When you can do it in both directions, work with a partner and clap it as a duet—one person working from left to right, the other person working from right to left.

45. RHYTHM CHALLENGE

(a & 4 3 & e 2 1)

PLAYING NOTES

Use what you've learned about sixteenth notes to play the melody for "Three Little Birds." After you pick the melody, learn the reggae strum shown below and play the song again, strumming and singing.

46. THREE LITTLE BIRDS

Words and Music by
Bob Marley

STRUM BUILDER 6

To strum the reggae style of "Three Little Birds," we'll use a downward strum on the "&" of every beat. This is called the "after-beat" or "upbeat." It will help to tap your foot on the beat as you learn this strum. You'll strum down each time your foot comes up.

PERFORMANCE SPOTLIGHT

47. OVER THE RAINBOW from THE WIZARD OF OZ

Music by Harold Arlen
Lyric by E.Y. "Yip" Harburg
As Performed by Israel Kamakawiwo'ole

PLAYING CHORDS

THEORY

Cut Time ₵ 2/2 "Count on Me" is written in **cut time**. This can also be seen as **2/2 time**. In this meter, there are two beats in a measure, and each half note receives one beat. This means that the length of each note duration is cut in half.

Count aloud as you clap the rhythm for each of these lines of rhythm.

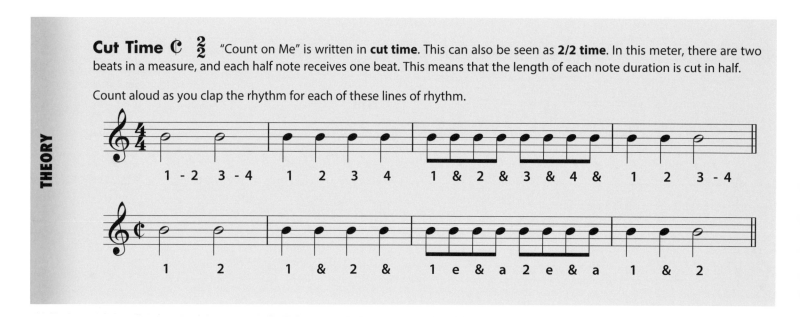

In order to get the cut-time feel, play "Count on Me" with just two downstrokes in each measure.

48. COUNT ON ME

Words and Music by Bruno Mars,
Ari Levine and Philip Lawrence

Pre-Chorus

We find out what __ we're made of when we __ __ are called __ to help __ our friends __ in need. You can

Chorus

count on me like "one, two, three." I'll be __ there. And I know when I need it, I can count on you like "four, three, two," and you'll be __ there, 'cause that's __ what friends __ are s'posed __ to do, __ oh yeah. Ooh, __ ooh, __ __ you can count __ on me, __ 'cause I __ can count on you. __

Strum Challenge

Now that you're used to the two-beat, cut-time feeling, go back and try this more complicated strum for "Count on Me."

For a different sound, use just your index finger to strum the strings. Strum down with the back of your fingernail and up with the fleshy tip of your finger.

1 & 2 e & a   1 & 2 e & a

PLAYING CHORDS

Use this simple strum to get the two-beat feeling of another cut-time song: "Everyday."

49. EVERYDAY

Words and Music by Norman Petty
and Charles Hardin

STRUM BUILDER 7

Use this two-measure strum pattern to play "Guantanamera."

PLADING CHORDS

50. GUANTANAMERA

Musical Adaptation by Pete Seeger and Julian Orbon
Lyric Adaptation by Julian Orbon, based on a poem by Jose Marti
Lyric Editor: Hector Angulo
Original Music and Lyrics by Jose Fernandez Diaz

HISTORY

Pete Seeger (1919–2014) helped to revive popular interest in the traditional folk music of the Americas. Throughout his long career as a musician, he used the power of songs to promote peace and justice. Although we know him best as a guitar and banjo player, he would frequently talk about how his life in music began when he learned to play the ukulele as a boy.

PERFORMANCE SPOTLIGHT

Use both rhythmic strumming and individual notes to play "Sloop John B."

51. SLOOP JOHN B. – Ukulele Solo

Traditional

PLAYING NOTES

Throughout this duet, the melody changes from one part to the other every four measures. Make sure that the parts are balanced in volume so that the melody can always be heard.

52. BARBARA ALLEN - Duet

Traditional English

HISTORY

Before the age of electronic communication, folk songs were passed from one singer to the next. As the songs moved gradually from one area to another, changes and variations were introduced to the melody and the words. Like many popular folk songs, there are several versions of the song "Barbara Allen" that emerged over time. The melody used in the duet above is the version that became popular in Scotland. Different melodies for "Barbara Allen" became well-known in Britain, Ireland, and the United States.

PLAYING CHORDS

UNDERSTANDING CHORDS – MINOR CHORDS

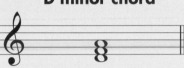

Pitches = **A D F A**

Minor chords are the third type of chord we've used while playing songs. A chord name that contains an upper case letter followed by a lower case "m" or the letters "min" refers to a minor chord.

Like a major chord, a minor chord is a **triad**, which means it contains three different pitches. On ukulele, there will always be one pitch of the minor chord that's doubled when all four strings are strummed.

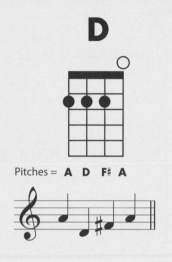

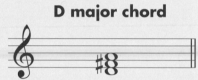

Pitches = **A D F♯ A**

D minor chord

Look at the difference between the D minor chord and the D major chord. In the minor chord, the middle note is lowered a half step from where it would be in the major chord.

Play each of these chords and listen to the difference in the sound. Minor chords are often described as sounding "darker" or "sadder" than major chords.

D major chord

This song uses several minor chords. Listen to the mood that these chords create and note the contrast in sound created when a major chord is played.

53. FOLLOW THE DRINKIN' GOURD

African-American Spiritual

Shuffle feel

Fol - low _____ the drink - ing gourd. _ Fol - low _____ the drink-ing gourd. _ For the

old man is a - wait-in' for to car - ry you to free-dom. Fol-low the drink - ing gourd.

HISTORY The song "Follow the Drinkin' Gourd" tells the story of the dangerous journey that was made by escaped slaves who traveled in secret on the underground railway. The constellation "the drinking gourd" is also known as the Big Dipper. The handle of the dipper points to the North Star. By traveling in the dark of night, the slaves could follow the star north, eventually finding their way to freedom.

PLACING CHORDS

Use this strum pattern to play "Scarborough Fair" and check out the Chord Chart on pages 46 and 47 to learn the A chord.

54. SCARBOROUGH FAIR

Traditional English

ESSENTIAL ELEMENTS QUIZ – Minor Chord Decoder

On the lines below the chord diagrams, write the names of the pitches that are being played on each string. Then write the notes on the staff. Remember that some chord notes will be doubled.

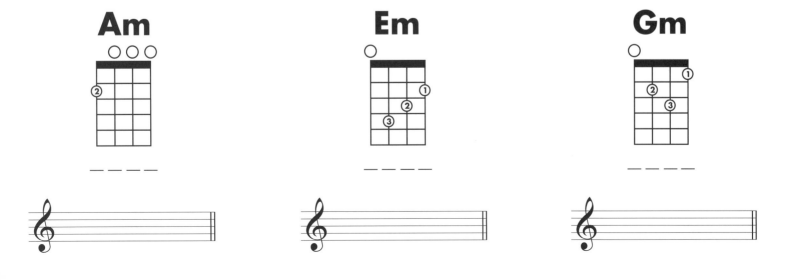

COUNTING

THEORY

Dotted Eighth Notes

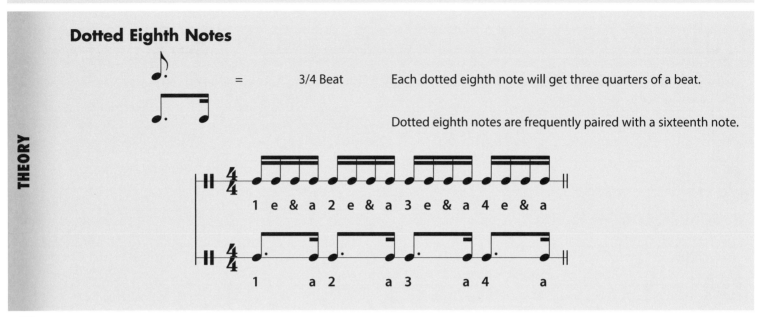

=   3/4 Beat   Each dotted eighth note will get three quarters of a beat.

Dotted eighth notes are frequently paired with a sixteenth note.

55. I'VE BEEN WORKING ON THE RAILROAD

American Folksong

56. SHALL WE GATHER AT THE RIVER?

Words and Music by
Robert Lowry

PLAYING CHORDS

Practice Tip

Play the melody for "Yellow Submarine" and then play the chords while singing the melody. Look through the song and make sure that you know the left-hand formation for all the chords. If you need a reminder of how to play any of the chords, look at the Chord Chart on pages 46 and 47.

57. YELLOW SUBMARINE

Words and Music by John Lennon
and Paul McCartney

PLAYING CHORDS

THEORY

A **coda** is an ending for a piece of music. The word comes from an Italian word meaning "tail."

D.S. al Coda or ***Dal Segno al Coda*** is an indication that you should repeat part of the music before playing the coda. There are four markers that are used to create the roadmap for the repeat and ending:

- Play from the beginning of the piece up to the ***D.S. al Coda*** marker.

- Go back to the 𝄋 sign (or "segno").

- Repeat all the measures up to the ***To Coda*** ⊕ marker.

- Jump to the ⊕ **Coda** symbol and play to the end of the piece.

Practice Tip

We'll use a two-measure strum pattern for "Upside Down."

There are places in "Upside Down" where the chords change within the strum pattern. Take a minute to practice those measures before you try the whole song.

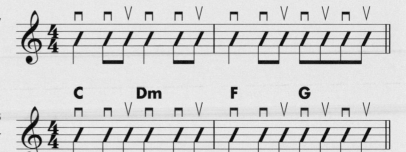

58. UPSIDE DOWN from the Universal Pictures and Imagine Entertainment film CURIOUS GEORGE

Words and Music by
Jack Johnson

PLAYING MOVEABLE CHORDS

THEORY

In Book 1, we learned that any chord shape that depresses all four strings can be moved up or down the fingerboard to any fret. This gives us lots of options for alternate chord formations that can add more interest to our chord progressions. Here's another moveable chord shape that works well in many songs.

 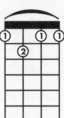 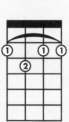  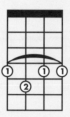 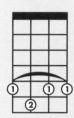

Each time you move up by one fret, the chord is one half step higher.

Practice Tip

Play the following exercise using the moveable chord position shown above. Work slowly so that you can check your left hand position. Listen to each chord change and make certain that you're getting an even tone from every string.

59. MOVING MOUNTAINS

We'll use this moveable formation to play some of the C7 and D7 chords in "Love Potion Number Nine." When the chord symbol is marked with a star (C7* or D7*), use the alternate, moveable form of the chord.

STRUM BUILDER 9

Use this strum for "Love Potion Number Nine."

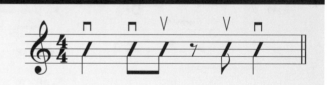

60. LOVE POTION NUMBER 9

Words and Music by Jerry Leiber
and Mike Stoller

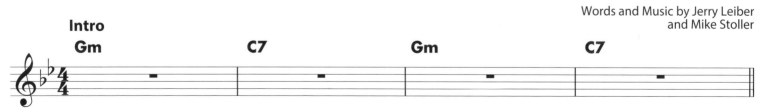

Verse

1. I took my trou-bles down to Ma-dam Ruth. __ You know, that gyp-sy with the
2. I told her that I was a flop with chicks. __ I've been that way since nine-teen-
3. I did-n't know if it was day or night. __ I start-ed kiss-in' ev-'ry-

gold - capped tooth. __ She's got a shop down at Thir - ty - fourth and Vine,
fif - ty - six. __ She looked at my palm and she made a mag - ic sign. She
thing in sight. __ But when I kissed a cop down at Thir - ty - fourth and Vine, he

sell - in' lit - tle bot - tles of
said, "What you need is
broke my lit - tle bot - tle of
Love Po - tion Num-ber Nine.

Nine."

She

Bridge

bent down and turned a - round and gave me a wink. __ She said, "I'm gon - na mix it up right

here in the sink." __ It smelled like tur - pen - tine, it looked like In - di - a ink. __ I

D.S. al Coda

Coda

held my nose, I closed my eyes, I took a drink!

Nine.

PLAYING MOVEABLE CHORDS

Use the moveable formation of the C chord to play "My Girl." Practice those measures first, before you play the whole song.

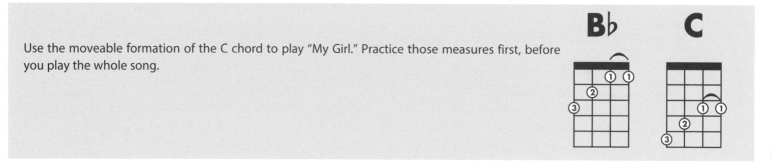

61. MY GIRL

Words and Music by William "Smokey" Robinson
and Ronald White

CHANGING STRINGS

Before you start, confirm that you've purchased strings that correctly match the size of your ukulele. Although standard (also called soprano), concert, and tenor ukuleles are all tuned the same, the strings for each size of instrument are slightly different.

Removing the Old Strings

- Take a minute to look at how the strings are attached at the bridge and which direction they wind onto the tuning pegs. You can take a picture to make certain.

- Turn the tuning key to completely loosen one string.

- Unwind the string from the tuning peg and untie the knot at the bridge.

- Repeat the process for each of the four strings.

Cleaning Your Ukulele

While you have the strings off, take advantage of this opportunity to clean your ukulele. Use a clean, soft, dry cloth to wipe down the front of the instrument. Clean between the tuning pegs, around the nut and bridge, and down the entire fingerboard.

Installing the New Strings

 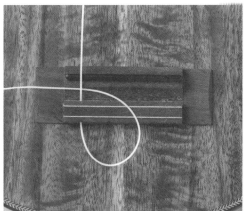 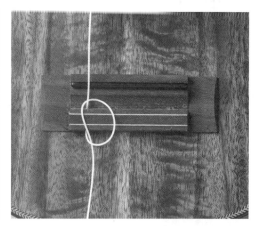

1. Pass the string through the hole in the bridge. You should have about three inches of string extending out of the bottom of the bridge.

2. Loosely wrap the short end of the string up over the bridge and around the long end of the string.

3. Wrap the string around itself.

4. Wrap the string around itself an additional turn or two.

5. Pull the short end of the string with one hand, and the long end with the other hand. Work the ends of the string gently back and forth until the knot draws tight.

6. Feed the long end of the string through the hole in the tuning peg. Wrap the string around the peg and back through the hole a second time.

7. Turn the tuning key to wind the string onto the peg and to bring the string up to pitch.

8. Carefully trim the extra from both ends of the string. A fingernail clipper works well for this job.

Tuning New Strings

Nylon ukulele strings need to stretch before they can properly stay in tune. It will be necessary to tune many times before your new strings become stable. One helpful trick is to tune your ukulele one half step higher than normal (G#, C#, F, A#) and let it sit overnight. When you take it back to normal tuning the next day, the strings will adjust more quickly.

CHORD CHART

As you learn new songs on your own, you will encounter chords that were not used in this book. You can use this chart to find the formations for many of those new chords. The chart includes the major, minor, and dominant seventh chord for each step of the scale.

	MAJOR	MINOR	DOM7
F#/G♭	**F#/G♭**	**F#m/G♭m**	**F#7/G♭7**
G	**G**	**Gm**	**G7**
G#/A♭	**G#/A♭**	**G#m/A♭m**	**G#7/A♭7**
A	**A**	**Am**	**A7**
A#/B♭	**B♭**	**A#m/B♭m**	**A#7/B♭7**
B	**B**	**Bm**	**B7**

STRUM CHART

Here are strum patterns that we've used throughout Book 2. As you learn new songs on your own, it may help to refer back to these rhythms. You can combine one-measure patterns to create your own two-measure strums.

One Measure Strum Patterns

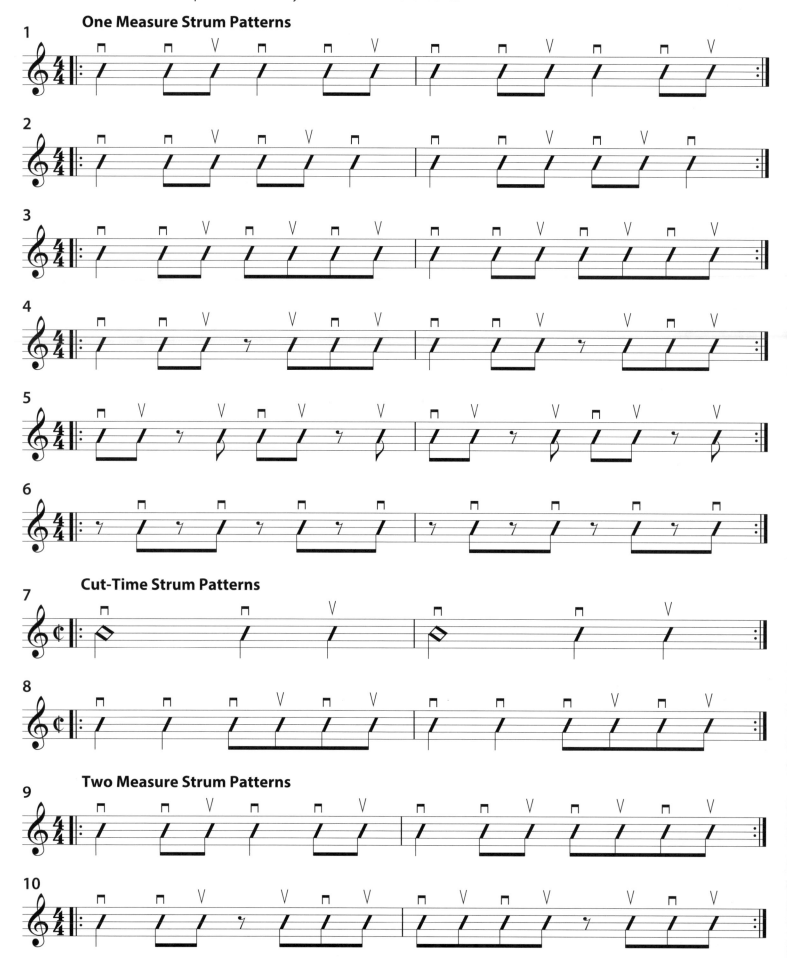

ESSENTIAL ELEMENTS

PIANO THEORY

ISBN 978-1-4768-0609-9

HAL•LEONARD®
CORPORATION

7777 W. BLUEMOUND RD. P.O. BOX 13819 MILWAUKEE, WI 53213

In Australia Contact:
Hal Leonard Australia Pty. Ltd.
4 Lentara Court
Cheltenham, Victoria, 3192 Australia
Email: ausadmin@halleonard.com.au

Visit Hal Leonard Online at
www.halleonard.com

To the Student

I wrote these books with you in mind. As a young student I often wondered how completing theory work-books would make me a better musician. The theory work often seemed separate from the music I was play-ing. My goal in *Essential Elements Piano Theory* is to provide you with the tools you will need to compose, improvise, play classical and popular music, or to better understand any other musical pursuit you might en-joy. In each "Musical Mastery" section of this book you will experience creative applications of the theory you have learned. The "Ear Training" pages will be completed with your teacher at the lesson. In this series you will begin to learn the building blocks of music, which make it possible for you to have fun at the piano. A practical understanding of theory enables you to see what is possible in music. I wish you all the best on your journey as you learn the language of music!

Sincerely,
Mona Rejino

To the Teacher

I believe that knowledge of theory is most beneficial when a concept is followed directly by a musical application. In *Essential Elements Piano Theory*, learning theory becomes far more than completing worksheets. Students have the opportunity to see why learning a particular concept can help them become a better pianist right away. They can also see how the knowledge of musical patterns and chord progressions will enable them to be creative in their own musical pursuits: composing, arrang-ing, improvising, playing classical and popular music, accompanying, or any other.

A free download of the *Teacher's Answer Key* is available at www.halleonard.com/eeptheory2answer.

Acknowledgements

I would like to thank Hal Leonard Corporation for providing me the opportunity to put these theoret-ical thoughts down on paper and share them with others. I owe a debt of gratitude to Jennifer Linn, who has helped with this project every step of the way. These books would not have been possible without the support of my family: To my husband, Richard, for his wisdom and amazing ability to solve dilemmas; to my children, Maggie and Adam, for helping me think outside the box.

TABLE OF CONTENTS

REVIEW

1. Complete writing the music alphabet going up two times.

    A _____ G

2. Circle all the sets of 2 black keys, then label each C D E group on the white keys.

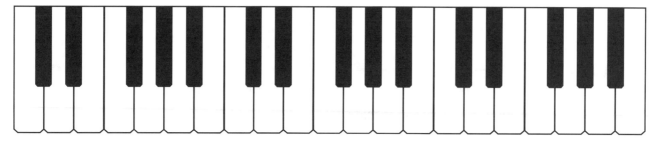

3. Circle all the sets of 3 black keys, then label each F G A B group on the white keys.

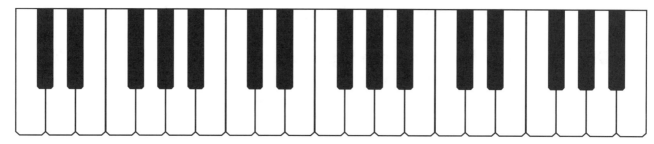

4. On the keyboard below, print the following six letter names on the correct white keys. *One key will be blank.*

    F   B   C   G   D   A

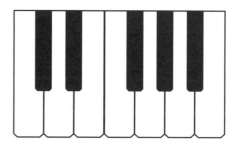

5. Write L under the line notes and S under the space notes.

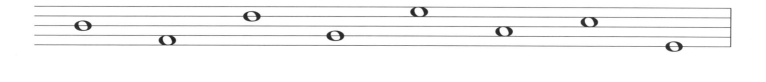

6. Circle the answer that shows the direction these notes move.

Step Up	Step Up	Step Up	Step Up
Step Down	Step Down	Step Down	Step Down
Repeat	Repeat	Repeat	Repeat

7. Add stems to these note heads. Follow the stem rule: *Stems go UP for notes below the middle line, and attach to the **right** side of the note head. Stems go DOWN for notes on or above the middle line, and attach to the **left** side of the note head.*

8. On this grand staff, trace the:
   a) brace
   b) bar line
   c) treble clef
   d) bass clef
   e) double bar line

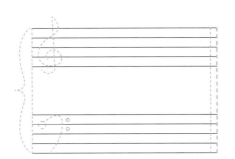

9. Add the missing parts to each grand staff below.

10. Draw a line connecting each note or rest to its name. Then draw a line connecting each name to the number of beats it receives in $\frac{4}{4}$ time.

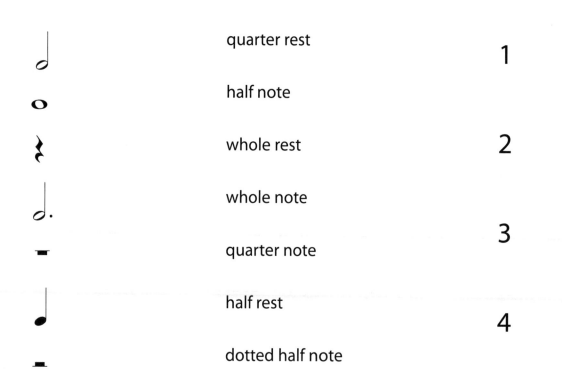

11. Add bar lines to each rhythm below. *The time signature will guide you.* Then write the counts below each measure.

Note Naming

1. The following notes either STEP or SKIP. Circle the correct answer for each example.

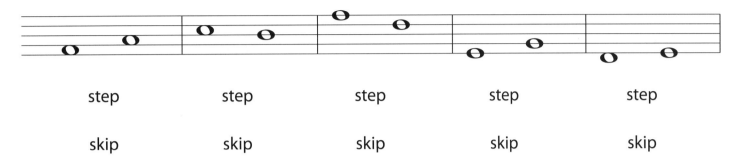

step   step   step   step   step

skip   skip   skip   skip   skip

2. Complete the notes stepping up the grand staff from Bass C to Treble C. Draw whole notes above each letter. *The Guide Notes are written for you.*

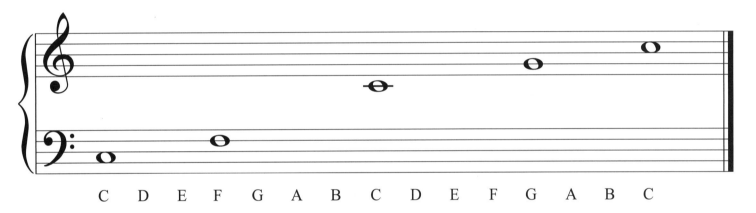

C   D   E   F   G   A   B   C   D   E   F   G   A   B   C

3. Fill in the blanks with the correct note names. Then draw a line from each note on the staff to its corresponding key on the keyboard.

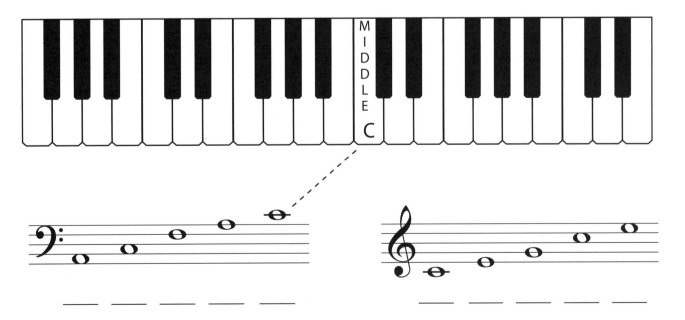

4. The following notes STEP UP or DOWN from Guide Notes. Fill in the blanks with the missing note names.

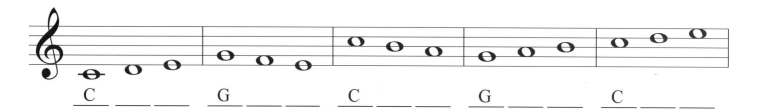

C ___ ___   G ___ ___   C ___ ___   G ___ ___   C ___ ___

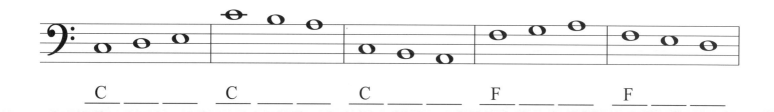

C ___ ___   C ___ ___   C ___ ___   F ___ ___   F ___ ___

5. The following notes SKIP UP or DOWN from Guide Notes. Fill in the blanks with the missing note names.

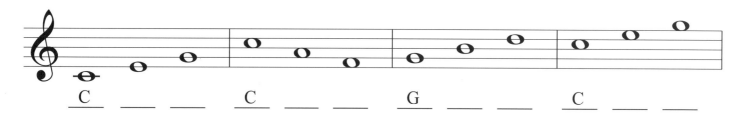

C ___ ___   C ___ ___   G ___ ___   C ___ ___

C ___ ___   F ___ ___   F ___ ___   C ___ ___

6. The following notes either STEP or SKIP from Guide Notes. Name each note.

___ ___ ___   ___ ___ ___   ___ ___ ___   ___ ___ ___

7. Name these notes. Each measure will spell a word.

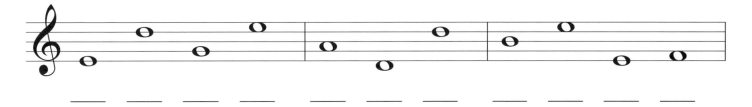

_____ _____ _____ _____   _____ _____ _____ _____   _____ _____ _____ _____

_____ _____ _____ _____   _____ _____ _____ _____ _____ _____ _____ _____

8. Spell these words by drawing whole notes on the treble staff.

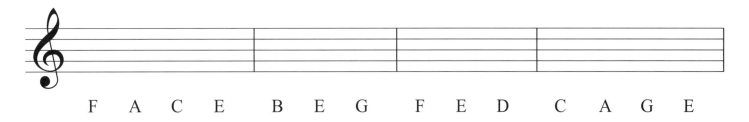

F A C E   B E G F   E D C A   G E

9. Spell these words by drawing whole notes on the bass staff.

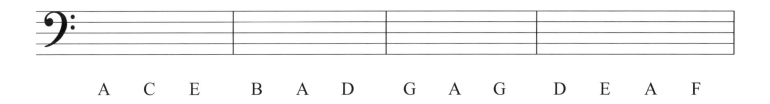

A C E   B A D   G A G   D E A F

10. Name the following notes on the grand staff. Each measure will spell a word.

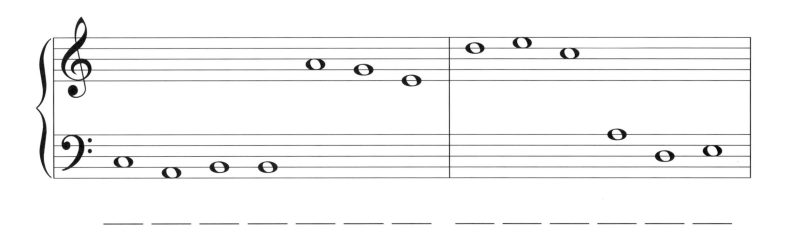

_____ _____ _____ _____ _____ _____   _____ _____ _____ _____ _____ _____

Musical Signs and Terms

DYNAMIC signs tell how soft or loud to play the music.

Italian Name	Sign (Symbol)	Meaning
piano	*p*	soft
mezzo piano	*mp*	medium soft
mezzo forte	*mf*	medium loud
forte	*f*	loud

1. Draw a line connecting each dynamic sign to its meaning.

mp	soft
f	medium loud
mf	medium soft
p	loud

TEMPO marks tell what speed to play the music.

Italian Name	Meaning
adagio	slow
andante	walking speed
moderato	moderate
allegro	fast (quickly and happily)

2. Draw a line connecting each tempo mark to its meaning.

andante	slow
allegro	walking speed
moderato	fast
adagio	moderate

Italian Name	Sign (Symbol)	Meaning
legato	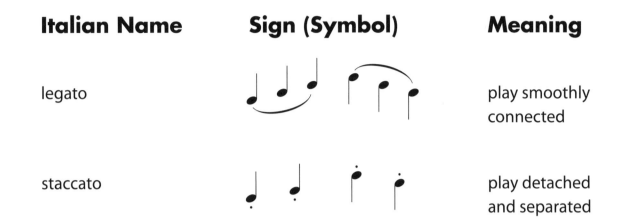	play smoothly connected
staccato		play detached and separated

Other Musical Symbols

D.C. al Fine means to return to the beginning (*da capo*) and play to *fine* (the end).

3. Clap the first four measures in the rhythm below. Return to the beginning (*capo*). Stop at the sign for the end (*fine*).

A **tie** is a curved line that connects notes of the same pitch. Play only the first note and hold it for the combined value of both notes.

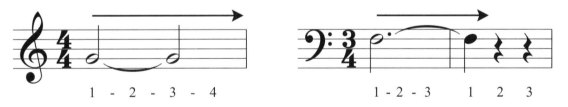

A **slur** is a curved line over or under two or more notes that are to be played *legato* (smoothly connected).

4. Draw a line connecting each musical term to its symbol, then connect each symbol to its meaning.

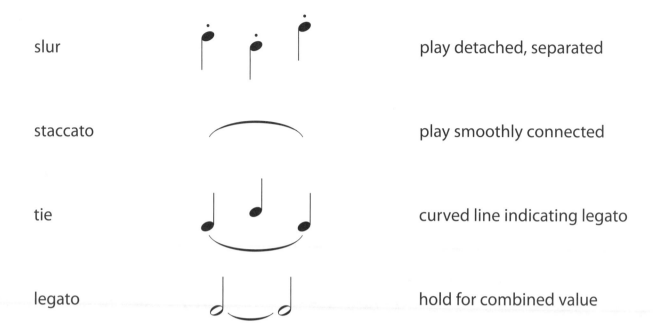

slur   play detached, separated

staccato   play smoothly connected

tie   curved line indicating legato

legato   hold for combined value

5. Write the total number of beats each pair of tied notes would receive.

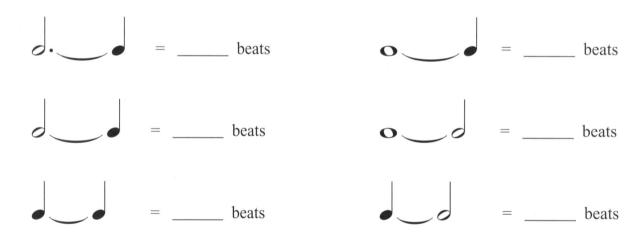

6. Write the word **tie** or **slur** to describe the curved line in each measure.

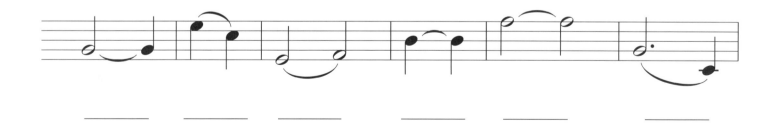

_____   _____   _____   _____   _____

MUSICAL MASTERY

Ear Training

1. Listen to the following rhythms. If they sound the same as what is written, circle SAME. If they sound different, circle DIFFERENT.

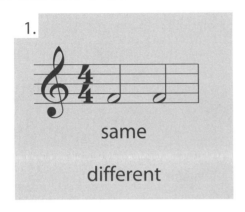

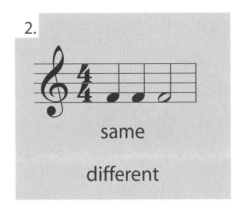

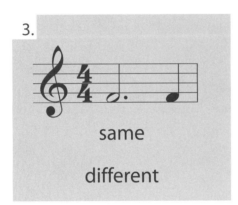

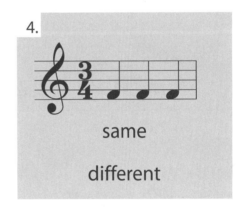

2. You will hear four groups of notes. Circle UP if the notes move up. Circle DOWN if the notes move down.

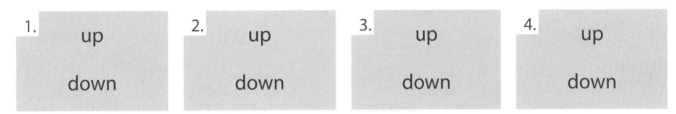

3. You will hear five groups of notes, with three notes in each group. The first two notes are written on the staff. Listen carefully, then write the third note in each measure.
   Hint: The third note will repeat, step up or step down.

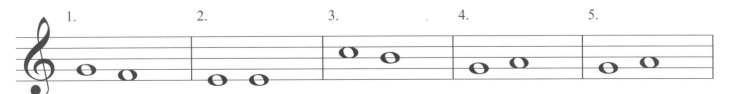

How's Your Italian?

You have learned many Italian words through your study of music. Some of these words describe the speed of the music. Some tell you what volume to play. Others describe how to play and release the keys.

1. Match each word in the box with its definition below. Then complete the crossword puzzle.

mezzo forte			forte	fine
	legato			
piano		adagio		moderato
andante			capo	
	mezzo piano			tempo
staccato		allegro		

Across

1. detached, separated

5. soft

7. medium loud

9. smoothly connected

12. slow tempo

13. moderate tempo

Down

2. walking tempo

3. rate of speed

4. fast tempo

6. medium soft

8. end

10. loud

11. return to the beginning

Musical Crossword Puzzle

5-Finger Pattern Improvisations

1. Write letter names on the keys to complete the 5-finger patterns.

C Major

G Major

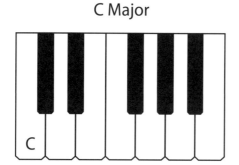
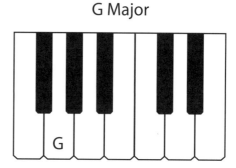

2. Draw quarter notes on the grand staff to complete the 5-finger patterns.
   Remember the stem rule.

3. Place both hands in the C Major 5-finger pattern in the upper range of the keyboard.
   As you hear the accompaniment below, improvise (make up) your own melody playing
   hands separately or together.

Accompaniment
(♩ = 80)

Repeat as desired   Last time

4. Place both hands in the G Major 5-finger pattern in the upper range of the keyboard.
   As you hear the accompaniment below, improvise (make up) your own melody playing
   hands separately or together.

Accompaniment
(♩ = 120)

Repeat as desired   Last time

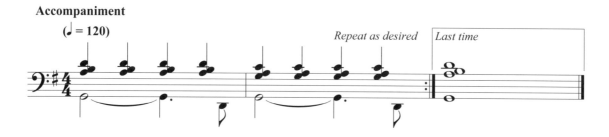

16

Rhythm and Time Signatures

1. Solve the music math equations by drawing the correct NOTE in the box.

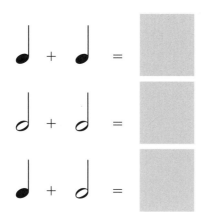

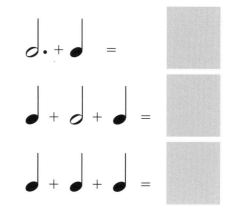

2. Write the number of counts each rest receives in $\frac{4}{4}$ time.

_____   _____   _____

3. Practice drawing rests on the staff. Trace each rest, then draw two more.

The QUARTER REST is placed in the middle of the staff.

The HALF REST sits on line 3.

The WHOLE REST hangs from line 4.

4. Add ONE NOTE to complete each measure. Notice the time signature.

5. Add ONE REST to complete each measure. Notice the time signature.

6. In the box, add the missing TIME SIGNATURE for each rhythmic example. Then write the counts below each measure.

7. Some measures below have the wrong number of counts. Draw an "X" through any measures that are incorrect.

Recognizing Intervals

An **INTERVAL** is the distance between two keys or notes.

Intervals on the keyboard include the first and last key, plus any keys skipped in between.

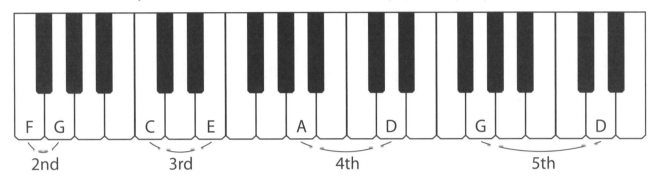

| 2nd | 3rd | 4th | 5th |

Intervals on the staff include the first and last note, plus any lines and spaces skipped in between.

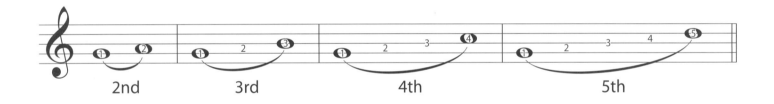

| 2nd | 3rd | 4th | 5th |

| 2nd | 3rd | 4th | 5th |

Interval of a 2nd = a step   Interval of a 3rd = a skip

2nds (steps)   3rds (skips)

1. Circle the correct answer for each pair of notes.

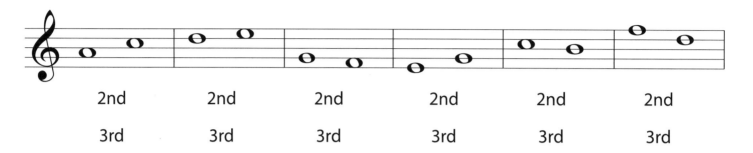

2nd	2nd	2nd	2nd	2nd	2nd
3rd	3rd	3rd	3rd	3rd	3rd

> Intervals that move from **line to space** or **space to line** are always even numbers.
>
> Intervals that move from **line to line** or **space to space** are always odd numbers.

2. In the box below each note, write L for line note and S for space note. In the blank, name the interval.

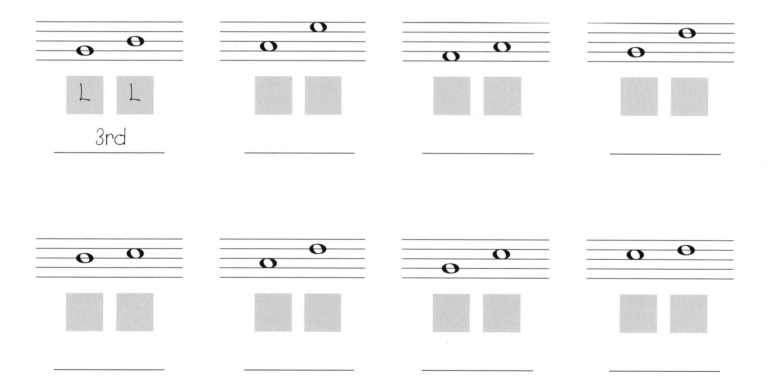

Intervals can be **MELODIC** or **HARMONIC**.

MELODIC INTERVALS are two notes played separately to make a melody.

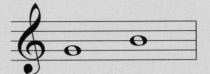

HARMONIC INTERVALS are two notes played together to make harmony.

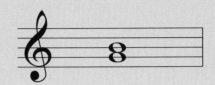

Melodic Intervals

| 2nd | 3rd | 4th | 5th |

Harmonic Intervals

| 2nd | 3rd | 4th | 5th |

3. In the box below each pair of notes, name the interval. In the blank, label the interval either melodic or harmonic.

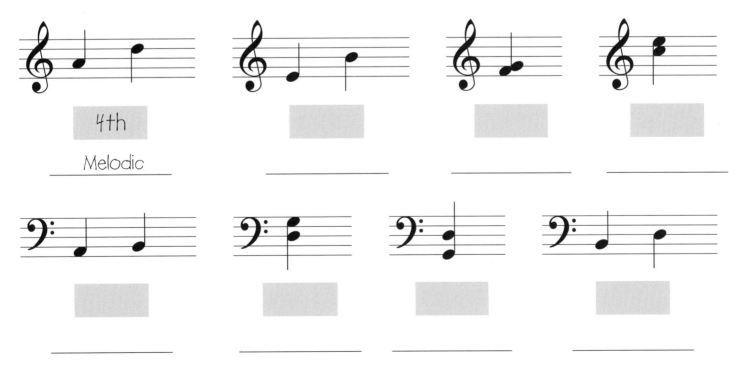

4th

Melodic

UNIT 6

Writing Intervals

1. Trace the whole notes on the grand staff below. Write the letter name for each note in the blank. *The notes are skipping up by intervals of a 3rd.*

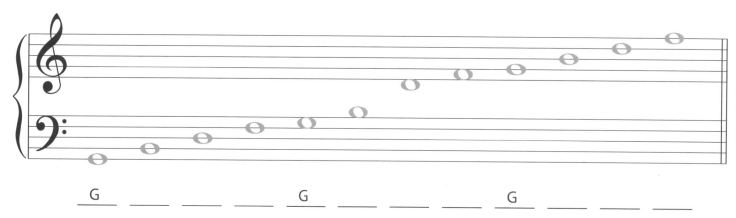

G _____ _____ G _____ _____ G _____ _____

2. What recurring 4-note pattern did you discover? _____ _____ _____ _____

3. Draw a melodic 2nd stepping up from the given note. Name each note.

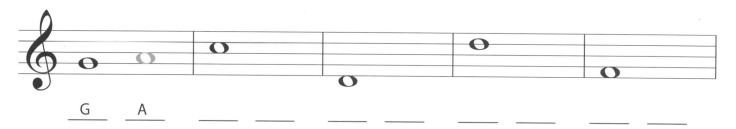

G   A

4. Draw a harmonic 2nd above each given note. *The notes will be touching side by side.*

5. Draw a melodic 3rd skipping up from the given note. Name each note.

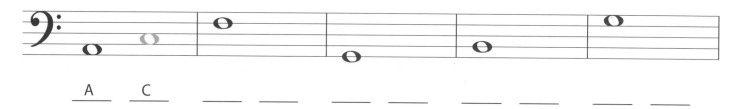

A   C

22

6. Draw a harmonic 3rd above each given note.

7. Draw a melodic 4th going up from the given note. Name each note.

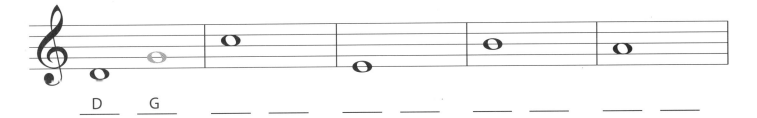

D   G   ___   ___   ___   ___   ___   ___   ___   ___

8. Draw a harmonic 4th above each given note.

9. Draw a melodic 5th going up from the given note. Name each note.

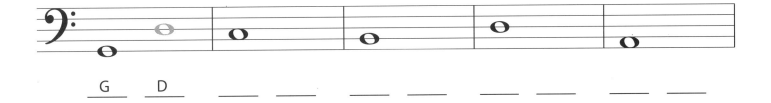

G   D   ___   ___   ___   ___   ___   ___   ___   ___

10. Draw a harmonic 5th above each given note.

MUSICAL MASTERY

Ear Training

1. You will hear four musical examples. Listen for the tempo (adagio or allegro), and the articulation (legato or staccato). Circle the Italian terms that match what you hear.

1.

Adagio	or	Allegro
Legato	or	Staccato

2.

Adagio	or	Allegro
Legato	or	Staccato

3.

Adagio	or	Allegro
Legato	or	Staccato

4.

Adagio	or	Allegro
Legato	or	Staccato

2. You will hear four musical examples in either $\frac{3}{4}$ or $\frac{4}{4}$ time. Listen closely, then circle the correct time signature.

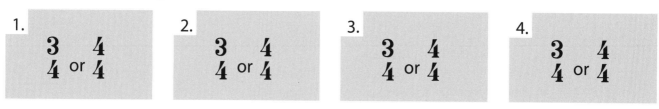

1. $\frac{3}{4}$ or $\frac{4}{4}$ 2. $\frac{3}{4}$ or $\frac{4}{4}$ 3. $\frac{3}{4}$ or $\frac{4}{4}$ 4. $\frac{3}{4}$ or $\frac{4}{4}$

3. You will hear three groups of melodies. Circle the pattern that matches what you hear.

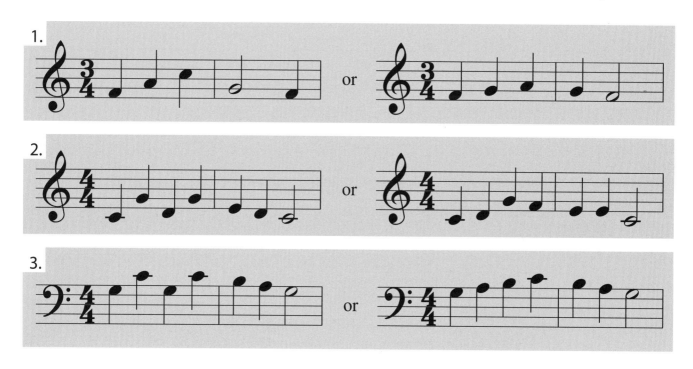

24

Interval Riddle

1. Play each clue on the keyboard. Write the name of the note you land on in the blank.

F – up a 2nd ___G___ 18   E – up a 4th _____ 3

G – down a 3rd _____ 4   B – down a 3rd _____ 5

D – up a 5th _____ 10   D – up a 2nd _____ 12

F – down a 4th _____ 2   F – down a 5th _____ 9

B – up a 3rd _____ 6   G – up a 2nd _____ 16

C – down a 2nd _____ 15   A – down a 4th _____ 19

A – up a 5th _____ 8   F – up a 5th _____ 11

D – down a 4th _____ 13   B – down a 2nd _____ 14

C – up a 3rd _____ 7   D – up a 4th _____ 1

F – down a 3rd _____ 17

2. To solve the riddle, transfer the numbered notes to their matching blanks below.

What are three things you might do at camp?

_____ o   _____ _____ n o _____ i n _____
 1   2   3   4   5

r i _____ _____   h o r s _____ _____ _____ _____ k
    6   7   8   9   10   11

_____ _____ r n   _____   _____ _____ _____ _____ _____
 12   13   14   15   16   17   18   19

25

Reading Mastery

1. Place your hands in the C Major 5-finger pattern. Play "Frère Jacques."

Frère Jacques

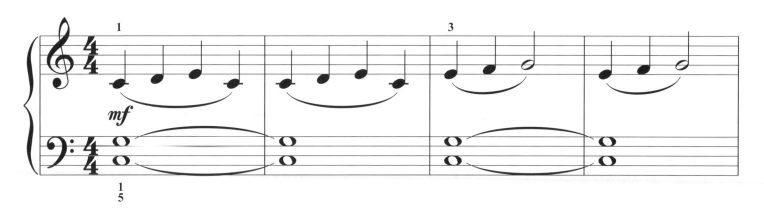

Playing a piece in a different position is called **TRANSPOSING**.

2. Transpose "Frère Jacques." Place your hands in the G Major 5-finger pattern. Keep the intervals and rhythms the same. Play "Frère Jacques" in the G Major 5-finger pattern.

Sharps, Flats and Naturals

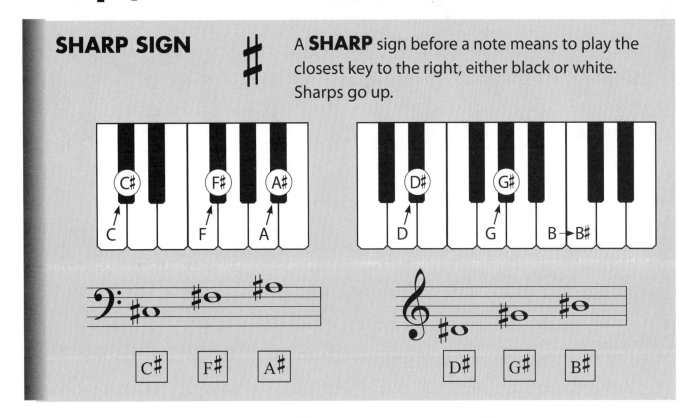

SHARP SIGN ♯ A **SHARP** sign before a note means to play the closest key to the right, either black or white. Sharps go up.

Sharps in Spaces   Sharps on Lines

1. Trace these sharps.

2. Draw a sharp before each note below. Then write the name of each note in the blank.

D♯ _____ _____ _____ _____ _____ _____

C♯ _____ _____ _____ _____ _____ _____

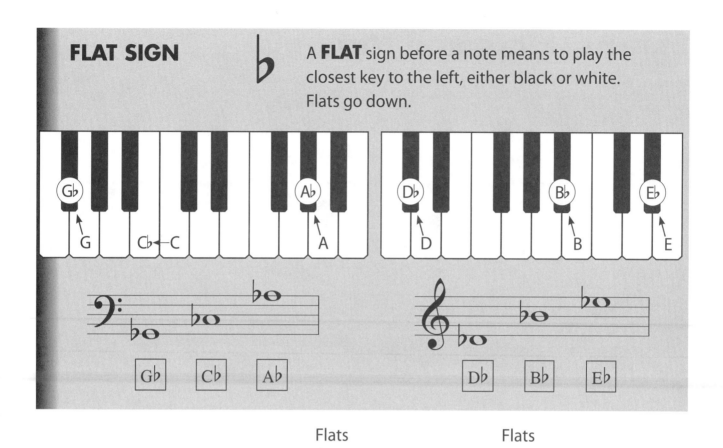

FLAT SIGN

A **FLAT** sign before a note means to play the closest key to the left, either black or white. Flats go down.

Flats in Spaces   Flats on Lines

3. Trace these flats.

4. Draw a flat before each note below. Then write the name of each note in the blank.

A♭ ___ ___ ___ ___ ___ ___ ___

G♭ ___ ___ ___ ___ ___ ___ ___

NATURAL SIGN

A **NATURAL** sign before a note cancels a sharp or flat. A natural is always a white key.

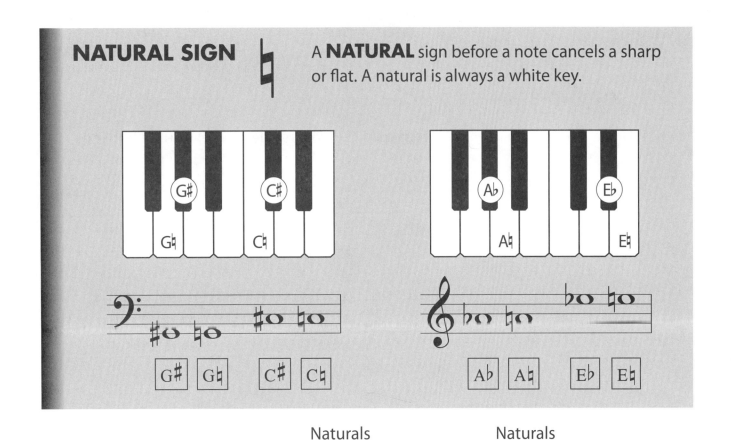

Naturals in Spaces Naturals on Lines

5. Trace these naturals.

6. Draw a natural before the second note in each measure. Then write the name of each note in the blank.

D♯   D♮

F♯   F♮

Review

1. Form a **GRAND STAFF** below by adding these parts:

   a) brace   b) bar line   c) treble clef   d) bass clef   e) double bar line

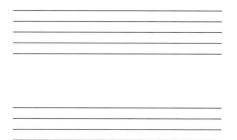

2. Fill in the blanks with the correct note names. Then draw a line connecting each note on the staff to its corresponding key on the keyboard.

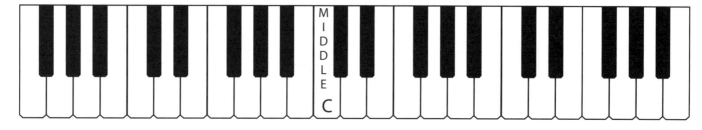

3. Solve the problems by writing the correct **number** in each box.

4. Add one **rest** to complete each measure. Notice the time signature.

5. Label each interval in the blank: 2nd, 3rd, 4th or 5th.

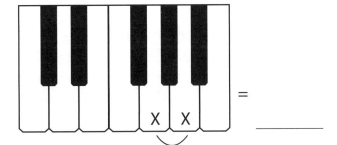 = _____

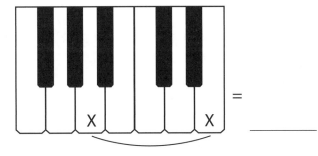 = _____

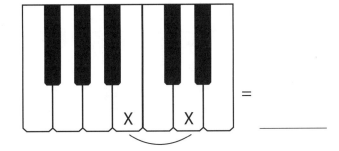 = _____

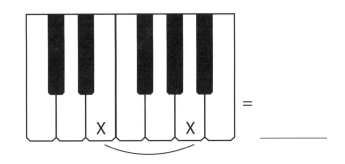 = _____

6. In the blanks below, arrange these dynamic signs in order from softest to loudest.

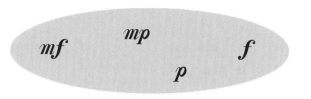

_____ _____ _____ _____

7. Follow the directions and draw **harmonic intervals** above or below the given note.

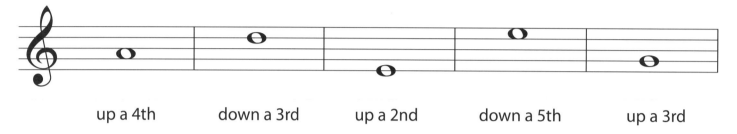

up a 4th   down a 3rd   up a 2nd   down a 5th   up a 3rd

8. Draw a line connecting each sharp or flat on the staff to its matching sharp or flat on the keyboard.

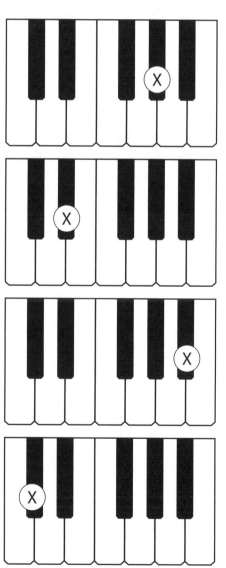

MUSICAL MASTERY

Ear Training

1. You will hear intervals of a 2nd (step) or a 3rd (skip). Each interval will be played in its melodic and harmonic form. Circle the interval you hear.

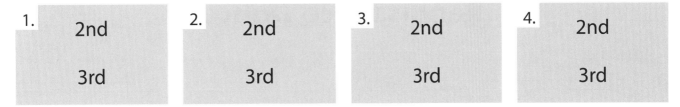

1. 2nd 3rd
2. 2nd 3rd
3. 2nd 3rd
4. 2nd 3rd

2. Listen to the following rhythms. If they sound the same as what is written, circle same. If they sound different, circle different.

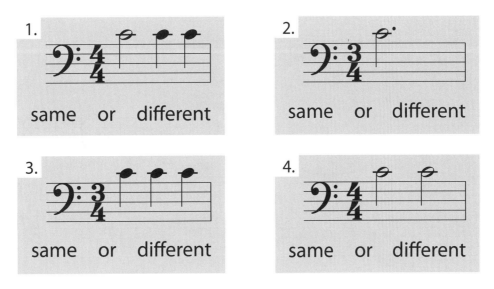

1. same or different
2. same or different
3. same or different
4. same or different

3. You will hear three groups of melodies. Circle the pattern that matches what you hear.

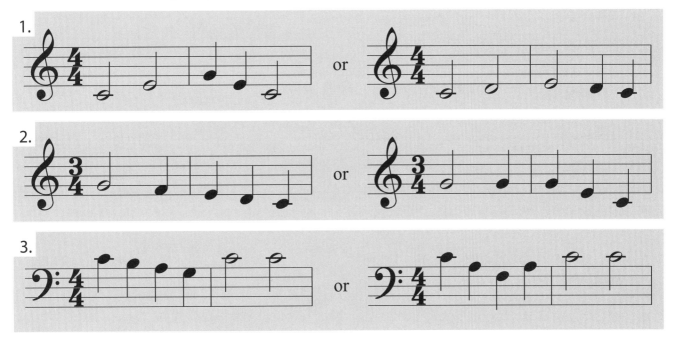

1. ___ or ___
2. ___ or ___
3. ___ or ___

Analysis

Study this excerpt from "Renaissance Dance," then read the statements about it below. Circle **true** if the statement is true, and **false** if the statement is false.

Renaissance Dance

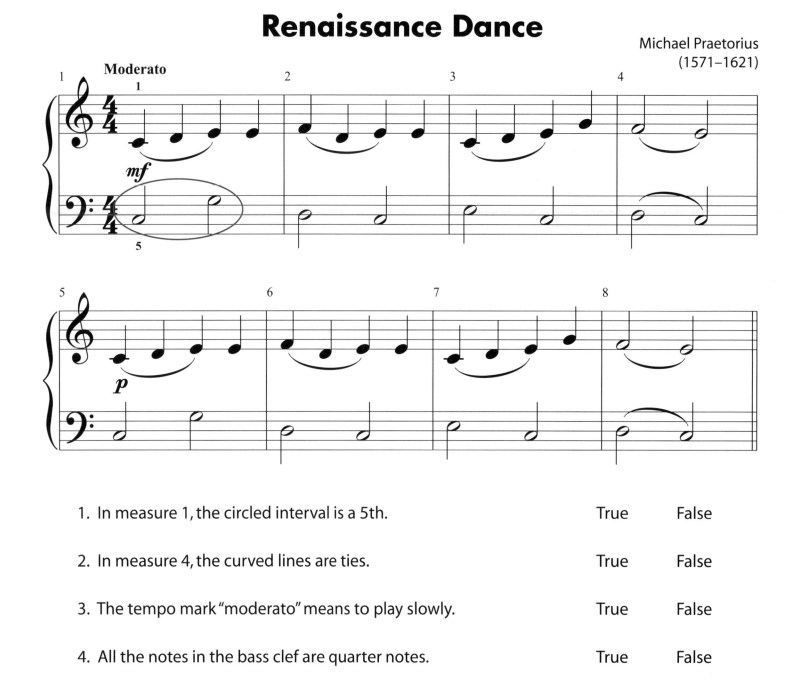

Michael Praetorius
(1571–1621)

1. In measure 1, the circled interval is a 5th.   True   False

2. In measure 4, the curved lines are ties.   True   False

3. The tempo mark "moderato" means to play slowly.   True   False

4. All the notes in the bass clef are quarter notes.   True   False

5. The dynamic mark _mf_ in measure 1
   means to play medium loud.   True   False

6. All the notes in measures 5–8 are the   True   False
   same as the notes in measures 1–4.

Symbol Mastery

1. Draw a line connecting each term in Column A with its symbol in Column B.
   Then draw a line connecting each symbol in Column B with its meaning in Column C.

Column A	Column B	Column C
tie		next key lower
	mp	
flat		hold for combined value
	(staccato notes)	
mezzo piano		medium soft
	(tied notes)	
staccato		detached, separated
	f	
forte		next key higher
	♭	
sharp		medium loud
	(slurred notes)	
legato		loud
	mf	
mezzo forte		cancels flat or sharp
	♯	
natural		smoothly connected
	p	
piano		soft
	♮	

35

THEORY MASTERY

Review Test

1. Starting with the letter A, write the music alphabet going up two times.

    ____ ____ ____ ____ ____ ____ ____ ____ ____ ____ ____ ____ ____ ____

2. Print these six letter names on the correct keys.

    Use only these letters: **C   E   B   F   D   A**

    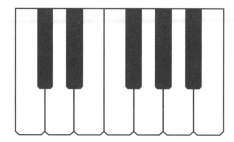

3. Print the letter name of each note in the blank. Each measure will spell a word.

    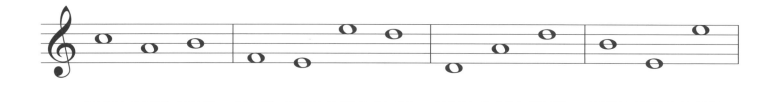

4. Spell these words by drawing whole notes on the bass staff.

    C A F E   F A D E   B E A D   E G G

5. Write the number of beats each note or rest gets in $\frac{4}{4}$ time.

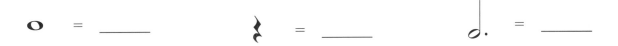

6. Draw the note or rest named below each measure.

Half Note   Quarter Rest   Whole Note

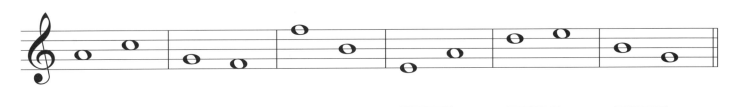

Whole Rest   Dotted Half Note   Half Rest

7. Fill in the blank with the name of the interval (2nd, 3rd, 4th or 5th).

8. On the staff below, circle the example with notes that move **up a 3rd** and **down a 2nd**.

37

9. Draw bar lines where they are needed below.

10. Write the counts below each note and each rest.

11. Circle the music symbol that matches the name given.

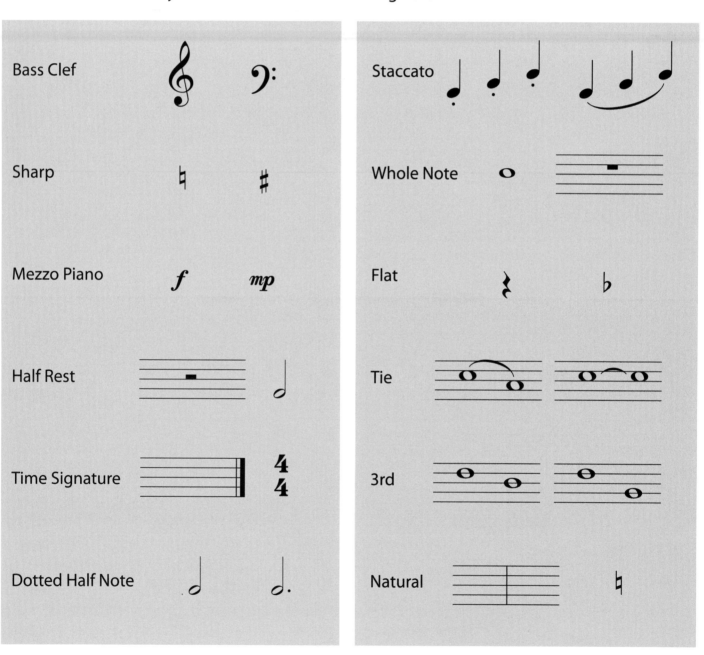

Ear Training

1. You will hear five groups of notes. Circle **up** if the notes move up. Circle **down** if the notes move down.

1.	2.	3.	4.	5.
up	up	up	up	up
down	down	down	down	down

2. Listen to the following rhythms. If they sound the same as what is written, circle **same**. If they sound different, circle **different**.

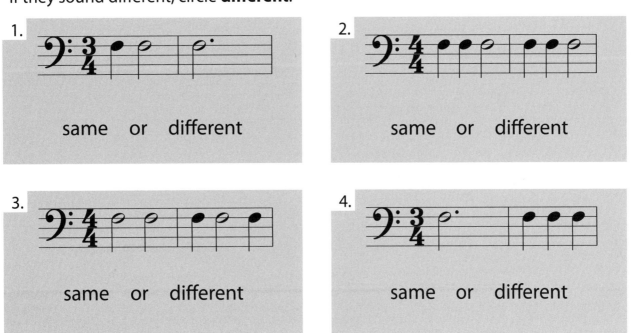

1.

same   or   different

2.

same   or   different

3.

same   or   different

4.

same   or   different

3. You will hear three notes in each group. The first two notes are written on the staff. After you hear the first two notes, write the missing third note on the staff.

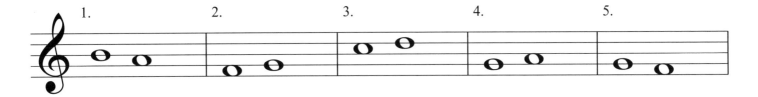